WHAT EATS WHAT IN A
FOREST
FOOD CHAIN

ILLUSTRATED BY **ZACK MCLAUGHLIN**   WRITTEN BY **LISA J. AMSTUTZ**

PICTURE WINDOW BOOKS
a capstone imprint

Every plant and animal in a forest is part of a food chain. In a food chain, energy moves from one living thing to the next.

In a forest, the trees are the first link in a food chain. They reach toward the sun. Almost all food chains need the sun's energy.

producer

Producers use sunlight, water, nutrients, and air to make their own food.

Plop! An acorn falls from the tree. An acorn weevil spies a crack. The weevil chews the seed inside.

 A consumer eats plants or animals for energy. An herbivore eats only plants.

consumer, herbivore

A hungry mouse spots the weevil. **Crunch!**
The mouse will save the acorn for later.

consumer,
omnivore

An omnivore eats both plants and animals.

9

A young snake coils nearby, waiting.

Gulp!

consumer,
carnivore

A carnivore eats only other animals.

Its belly full, the snake
finds a spot to rest.

consumer,
omnivore

Later a raccoon rambles down to the river.
It spots dinner and swipes. The snake makes a good meal.

The raccoon heads back to its den.
A bobcat waits quietly in the trees.

Pounce! The cat attacks.

consumer,
carnivore

15

The bobcat is a great hunter. But one day the bobcat is hurt in a fight with another cat. The wound is deadly.

A vulture feeds on parts of the bobcat's body.

consumer,
scavenger

A scavenger eats mainly dead plants or animals.

17

Worms, bacteria, and fungi break down the rest.
The decomposers return nutrients to the soil.

decomposers

Decomposers break down dead plants and animals. Their waste is used as nutrients by plants.

19

In spring an acorn sprouts. It uses the nutrients in the soil to grow.

A new oak tree reaches for the sun. And the food chain goes on.

FOOD WEB

You've seen a food chain in action. Now take a look at this temperate deciduous forest food web. A food web is made up of many food chains in one area.

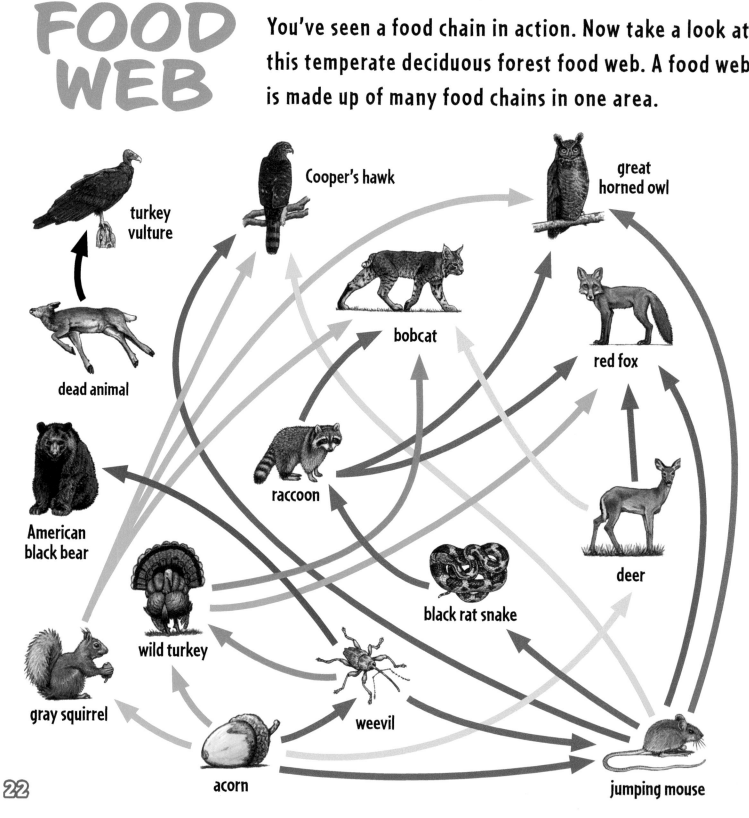

turkey vulture

Cooper's hawk

great horned owl

dead animal

bobcat

red fox

American black bear

raccoon

black rat snake

deer

wild turkey

weevil

gray squirrel

acorn

jumping mouse

GLOSSARY

bacteria—tiny living things that exist all around you and in you; some bacteria cause disease

carnivore—an animal that eats only other animals

consumer—an animal that eats plants or animals for energy

decomposer—a living thing, such as fungi or bacteria, that breaks down dead plants or animals

food web—many food chains connected to one another

fungus—a living thing similar to a plant but without leaves, flowers, or roots

herbivore—an animal that eats only plants

nutrient—part of food, like a vitamin, that is used for growth

omnivore—an animal that eats both plants and animals

producer—a plant that uses sunlight, water, nutrients, and air to grow

scavenger—an animal that feeds mainly on dead plants or animals

READ MORE

Fleisher, Paul. *Forest Food Webs.* Early Bird Food Webs. Minneapolis: Lerner Publications Co., 2008.

Salas, Laura Purdie. *Temperate Deciduous Forests: Lands of Falling Leaves:* Amazing Science. Minneapolis: Picture Window Books, 2007.

Vogel, Julia. *Deciduous Forest Food Chains.* Fascinating Food Chains. Edina, Minn.: Magic Wagon, 2011.

INTERNET SITES

FactHound offers a safe, fun way to find Internet sites related to this book. All of the sites on FactHound have been researched by our staff.

Here's all you do:

Visit *www.facthound.com*

Type in this code 9781404873889

Super-cool stuff!

Check out projects, games and lots more at
www.capstonekids.com

INDEX

LOOK FOR ALL THE BOOKS IN THE FOOD CHAINS SERIES:

WHAT EATS WHAT IN A
DESERT FOOD CHAIN

WHAT EATS WHAT IN A
FOREST FOOD CHAIN

WHAT EATS WHAT IN A
RAIN FOREST FOOD CHAIN

WHAT EATS WHAT IN AN
OCEAN FOOD CHAIN

Thanks to our advisers for their expertise, research, and advice:
John D. Krenz, PhD, Department of Biological Sciences
Minnesota State University, Mankato

Terry Flaherty, PhD, Professor of English
Minnesota State University, Mankato

Editor: Shelly Lyons
Designer: Alison Thiele
Art Director: Nathan Gassman
Production Specialist: Danielle Ceminsky
The illustrations in this book were created with Acrylic paint.

Picture Window Books
1710 Roe Crest Drive
North Mankato, MN 56003
www.capstonepub.com

Library of Congress Cataloging-in-Publication Data
Amstutz, Lisa J.
  What eats what in a forest food chain / by Lisa J. Amstutz ;
illustrations by Zack McLaughlin.
      p. cm.—(Capstone Picture Window Books: food chains)
  Includes index.
ISBN 978-1-4048-7388-9 (library binding)
ISBN 978-1-4048-7692-7 (paperback)
ISBN 978-1-4048-7982-9 (ebook PDF)
1. Forest ecology—Juvenile literature. 2. Forest
animals—Juvenile literature. 3. Food chains (Ecology)—Juvenile
literature. I. McLaughlin, Zack. II. Title.

QH541.5.F6A48 2013
577.3—dc23

                              2012001134

Printed in the United States   5657